Home
ORGANIZATION
TEAR OUTS *for the*
Whole Family

Get Everyone Mobilized to Organize Your Home
with 100 Printed Forms, Lists, Schedules and Directions

KRISTI DOMINGUEZ

founder of I Should Be Mopping the Floor

PAGE STREET
PUBLISHING CO.

PAGE STREET
PUBLISHING CO.

First published in 2016 by
Page Street Publishing Co.
27 Congress Street, Suite 105
Salem, MA 01970
www.pagestreetpublishing.com

Distributed by Macmillan, sales in Canada by The Canadian Manda Group.

19   18   17   16   1   2   3   4   5

ISBN-13: 978-1-62414-285-7
ISBN-10: 1-62414-285-0

Library of Congress Control Number: 2016936321

Cover and book design by Page Street Publishing Co.
Tear out designs by Kristi Dominguez

Printed and bound in China

Page Street is proud to be a member of 1% for the Planet. Members donate one percent of their sales to one or more of the over 1,500 environmental and sustainability charities across the globe who participate in this program.

DEDICATION

This book is dedicated to all of those other mediocre perfectionists who find organization a bit overwhelming at times. I feel your pain and struggle in the trenches. I also dedicate this to the three guys in my life...David, Benjamin and Jonathan. Because without their chaotic awesomeness, I'm not sure I would have ever been prompted to work so hard at home organization. Wink.

Contents

INTRODUCTION

If you've opened this book, chances are you're contemplating the chore of organizing. Whether you have a little project to organize, or you want to declutter, reinvent your entire home and how you live in it, this book is a practical companion for your journey.

As the saying goes, "A place for everything, and everything in its place—"; I'd love to take it further and add, "—and labeled perfectly." Because, who doesn't love a pretty label?

The prints in this book are the perfect way to put a fun spin on the sometimes daunting task of organization. There is a modern palette and similar feel to the designs in this book to give them a cohesive look—which can carry over and fit seamlessly into all styles of home décor. Cohesion is perfect for the visual part of organization.

You can remove the prints from their perforation and use in any manner you see fit (although there are suggestions with each print). Many will work well with lamination, dry erase markers and even magnets on the back. The best part? You can make copies of any of these prints. Need 100 pantry labels? Go for it!

I hope the organization tools you find in this book make your home a little brighter, happier, prettier—and, of course, better organized.

Kristi Dominguez

Other items to use with this book:

- → scissors
- → double-sided tape
- → dry-erase markers
- → permanent markers

- → self-laminating sheets
- → peel & stick magnets
- → 8 x 10-inch (20 x 25-cm) frame(s)

one

ORGANIZING YOUR DETAILS

It's all the little details that make life run a bit smoother. From a handy place to keep all of your online passwords, to a list of important numbers you may need at a moment's notice—details can turn into bigger issues quickly. To keep all of those details organized, this chapter is full of all the prints that you can use to create a home organization binder. From insurance information to family and friends' birthday lists—I didn't leave out a single detail.

(continued)

one

ORGANIZING
YOUR DETAILS (CONT.)

IMPORTANT DATES TO REMEMBER

JANUARY	FEBRUARY	MARCH

APRIL	MAY	JUNE

JULY	AUGUST	SEPTEMBER

OCTOBER	NOVEMBER	DECEMBER

Important Numbers

PHONE NUMBERS TO KNOW ➤

Primary Care Physician: _____ Phone: _____

Pediatrician: _____ Phone: _____

Hospital: _____ Phone: _____

Urgent Care: _____ Phone: _____

Dentist: _____ Phone: _____

Veterinarian: _____ Phone: _____

Pharmacy: _____ Phone: _____

In Case of Emergency Contact: _____ Phone: _____

In Case of Emergency Contact: _____ Phone: _____

Nearby Friend: _____ Phone: _____

Nearby Friend: _____ Phone: _____

Poison Control: _____ Phone: _____

Police Department: _____ Phone: _____

Fire Department: _____ Phone: _____

Other: _____ Phone: _____

Other: _____ Phone: _____

FAMILY INSURANCE INFORMATION ➤

Health Insurance Provider: _____ Policy Number: _____

Phone: _____ Group Number: _____

Home Insurance Provider: _____ Policy Number: _____

Phone: _____ Group Number: _____

Auto Insurance Provider: _____ Policy Number: _____

Phone: _____ Group Number: _____

Utilities & Service Accounts

Electric Provider: _____

Account Number: _____

Business Number: _____

Emergency Number: _____

Additional Number: _____

Gas Provider: _____

Account Number: _____

Business Number: _____

Emergency Number: _____

Additional Number: _____

Water Provider: _____

Account Number: _____

Business Number: _____

Emergency Number: _____

Additional Number: _____

Trash Provider: _____

Account Number: _____

Business Number: _____

Emergency Number: _____

Additional Number: _____

Sewer Provider: _____

Account Number: _____

Business Number: _____

Emergency Number: _____

Additional Number: _____

Waste Management: _____

Account Number: _____

Business Number: _____

Emergency Number: _____

Additional Number: _____

Internet Provider: _____

Account Number: _____

Business Number: _____

Emergency Number: _____

Additional Number: _____

Cable/TV Provider: _____

Account Number: _____

Business Number: _____

Emergency Number: _____

Additional Number: _____

Phone Provider: _____

Account Number: _____

Business Number: _____

Emergency Number: _____

Additional Number: _____

Cell Phone Service: _____

Account Number: _____

Business Number: _____

Emergency Number: _____

Additional Number: _____

PASSWORDS
and usernames

WEBSITE/URL	USERNAME	PASSWORD

Holiday Address List

Name: _____
Address: _____
_____
_____
Card: _____ Gift: _____

Name: _____
Address: _____
_____
_____
Card: _____ Gift: _____

Name: _____
Address: _____
_____
_____
Card: _____ Gift: _____

Name: _____
Address: _____
_____
_____
Card: _____ Gift: _____

Name: _____
Address: _____
_____
_____
Card: _____ Gift: _____

Name: _____
Address: _____
_____
_____
Card: _____ Gift: _____

Name: _____
Address: _____
_____
_____
Card: _____ Gift: _____

Name: _____
Address: _____
_____
_____
Card: _____ Gift: _____

Name: _____
Address: _____
_____
_____
Card: _____ Gift: _____

Name: _____
Address: _____
_____
_____
Card: _____ Gift: _____

Name: _____
Address: _____
_____
_____
Card: _____ Gift: _____

Name: _____
Address: _____
_____
_____
Card: _____ Gift: _____

BINDER CONTENTS:

BINDER CONTENTS:

BINDER CONTENTS:

BINDER CONTENTS:

1.5-inch (3.8-cm) Binder Spine Labels

NOTES

JANUARY	
FEBRUARY	
MARCH	
APRIL	
MAY	
JUNE	
JULY	
AUGUST	
SEPTEMBER	
OCTOBER	
NOVEMBER	
DECEMBER	
SUNDAY	
MONDAY	
TUESDAY	
WEDNESDAY	
THURSDAY	
FRIDAY	
SATURDAY	

file folder tabs by months & days ~ extra blank tabs

IMPORTANT ADDRESSES	VEHICLE TITLES
IMPORTANT DATES	VEHICLE SERVICE INFO
HOLIDAY CARD LIST	MEDICAL RECORDS
CHECKING ACCOUNTS	PRESCRIPTION INFO
SAVINGS ACCOUNTS	INSURANCE: HEALTH
LOAN INFO	INSURANCE: LIFE
CREDIT CARD STATEMENTS	INSURANCE: HOMEOWNER'S
ANNUITIES	INSURANCE: DISABILITY
RECORDS OF BONDS	BIRTH CERTIFICATES
RECORDS OF STOCKS	LEGAL DOCUMENTS
OTHER INVESTMENTS	RECEIPTS
PAST TAX RETURNS	WILLS
CURRENT TAX INFO	WARRANTIES
MORTGAGE INFO	MANUALS
LEASE/RENT INFO	EDUCATION INFO
MONTHLY BILLS	PET PAPERWORK
PAY STUBS	TRAVEL REWARDS INFO
RETIREMENT INFO	TRAVEL DOCUMENTS
EMPLOYMENT BENEFITS	OTHER INFO

file folder tabs by subject

file box labels

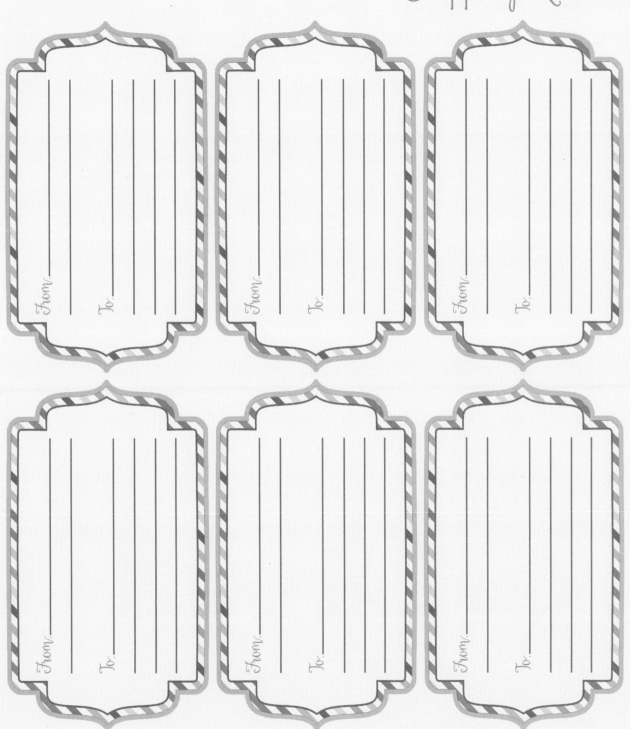

two

SYSTEMIZING YOUR DAILY LIFE

Daily planning is at the center of all organization. While having every minute of life scripted isn't anyone's idea of a good time, having general knowledge of what will happen throughout the day, week and month helps to keep us on task (and on time). This chapter includes a colorful array of super user-friendly calendars (daily, weekly and monthly), as well as a lovely assortment of to-do lists that will quickly turn into ta-da lists!

(continued)

two

SYSTEMIZING YOUR DAILY LIFE (CONT.)

Ahhh the to-do list. Kind of like the center of all organizational awesomeness, right? From little tasks to big ones, a running to-do list is an organized person's BFF. The best part is when it becomes your TA-DA list! Laminate or frame for use with a dry-erase marker.

Some of us like to make sure we're keeping track of everything that goes into our bodies. And honestly, all of us may benefit by giving this a try (it may surprise you). Use this print to write down every last bite and sip. Laminate or frame for use with a dry-erase marker.

Take the Weekly Food Log a step further by tracking your workouts and water, too. This is a fabulous health tool to keep yourself on track (and in the gym!). Laminate or frame for use with a dry-erase marker.

Did you know that, statistically, we're more likely to succeed with our goals if they're written down? Use this print and place it in a prominent spot to work toward achieving your monthly goals, whether they're personal, business, financial or whatever! You CAN and you WILL achieve those goals! Boom.

today's agenda ←————

THIS MORNING:	THIS AFTERNOON:
○	○
○	○
○	○
○	○
○	○
○	○
○	○
○	○
○	○
○	○
○	○
○	○
○	○
○	○

today's schedule

6:00 AM

7:00 AM

8:00 AM

9:00 AM

10:00 AM

11:00 AM

12:00 PM

1:00 PM

2:00 PM

3:00 PM

4:00 PM

5:00 PM

6:00 PM

7:00 PM

8:00 PM

This Week's Schedule

NOTES

MONDAY

TUESDAY

WEDNESDAY

THURSDAY

FRIDAY

SATURDAY

SUNDAY

Monthly Schedule

SUNDAY	MONDAY	TUESDAY	WEDNESDAY	THURSDAY	FRIDAY	SATURDAY

Weekly FOOD JOURNAL

	SUNDAY	MONDAY	TUESDAY	WEDNESDAY	THURSDAY	FRIDAY	SATURDAY
BREAKFAST:							
SNACK:							
LUNCH:							
SNACK:							
DINNER:							
SNACK:							
NOTES:							

Healthy Eating & Fitness Schedule

SUNDAY
Breakfast: _____
Lunch: _____
Dinner: _____
Snacks: _____

Water Intake: 💧💧💧💧 💧💧💧💧

Workout: _____
_____
Duration: _____

MONDAY
Breakfast: _____
Lunch: _____
Dinner: _____
Snacks: _____

Water Intake: 💧💧💧💧 💧💧💧💧

Workout: _____
_____
Duration: _____

TUESDAY
Breakfast: _____
Lunch: _____
Dinner: _____
Snacks: _____

Water Intake: 💧💧💧💧 💧💧💧💧

Workout: _____
_____
Duration: _____

WEDNESDAY
Breakfast: _____
Lunch: _____
Dinner: _____
Snacks: _____

Water Intake: 💧💧💧💧 💧💧💧💧

Workout: _____
_____
Duration: _____

THURSDAY
Breakfast: _____
Lunch: _____
Dinner: _____
Snacks: _____

Water Intake: 💧💧💧💧 💧💧💧💧

Workout: _____
_____
Duration: _____

FRIDAY
Breakfast: _____
Lunch: _____
Dinner: _____
Snacks: _____

Water Intake: 💧💧💧💧 💧💧💧💧

Workout: _____
_____
Duration: _____

SATURDAY
Breakfast: _____
Lunch: _____
Dinner: _____
Snacks: _____

Water Intake: 💧💧💧💧 💧💧💧💧

Workout: _____
_____
Duration: _____

three

REGULATING YOUR FINANCES

As the old adage goes, if you fail to plan, you plan to fail. This can be applied to all facets of life, but most definitely the b-word: BUDGET. While organizing finances can seem overwhelming and, well, downright terrifying to some, it can yield the rewards of keeping your money in check (and in your pocketbook). From trackable daily spending sheets to monthly budget sheets, this chapter is packed with all things money-related, with a friendly, non-scary approach.

(continued)

three

REGULATING
YOUR FINANCES (CONT.)

MONTHLY FINANCIAL GOALS   61

Monthly financial goals are just as important as the yearly ones—and can also be closely related to them. Perhaps you can obtain those larger yearly financial goals by breaking them up into 12 easier-to-achieve portions? Writing the smaller goals down in a spot you'll see often makes them that much easier to achieve. After crossing a few of these off your list, you'll be well on your way to crossing off the yearly financial goals, too.

YEARLY FINANCIAL GOALS   63

Just like in the previous chapter, we're more likely to succeed with our goals if they're written down. Yearly financial goals are important to keep track of, too. Whether you're trying to reach a certain figure in your savings account, save up for a large purchase or start college accounts for kids—pen to paper makes these goals that much more achievable. Be sure to post this one in a place where you'll be reminded of it often. Feel free to frame or laminate to use with a dry-erase marker.

BILL PAYMENT TRACKER   65

Ever get a few days past bill paying to realize you forgot one? Yeah, me too. HA! For all of us who experience the occasional forgetfulness in this area, this tracker is perfection. Every bill. Every month. Listed out in plain sight to check off as they're paid. Bada Bing Bada Boom. Laminate or frame to use over and over every month.

BANK ACCOUNT INFORMATION   67

If you use more than one financial institution, it may be a good idea to have them written down safely for your family, in case of emergency. This may be one to do in permanent ink so it can't be easily erased. In Chapter One (page 7), we talk about creating a Home Binder with lots of helpful information. This may be the spot where you'd like to keep your Bank Account Info page as well.

DEBT TRACKER PAYDOWN WORKSHEET   69

Let's face it: Debt stinks. But tackling it doesn't have to. Copy and use as many of these for the number of debts you're ready to face head-on—and watch them start to disappear one by one.

HOLIDAY BUDGET PLANNER   71

Just winging it through the holiday season can make for a rough new year if we're not careful, right? Plan the holidays long before they sneak up on you with this handy holiday budget print. There are common items listed, but also space to add your own personal expenses.

DAILY EXPENSE *tracker*

DATE	CATEGORY	DESCRIPTION	AMOUNT

WEEKLY EXPENSE *tracker*

DATE	CATEGORY	DESCRIPTION	AMOUNT

MONTHLY BUDGET *planner*

EARNINGS	EXPECTED AMOUNT	ACTUAL AMOUNT	DIFFERENCE
Income #1			
Income #2			

SAVINGS	EXPECTED AMOUNT	ACTUAL AMOUNT	DIFFERENCE
Emergency Fund			
Retirement			
Education			

HOME EXPENSES	EXPECTED AMOUNT	ACTUAL AMOUNT	DIFFERENCE
Mortgage/Rent			
Insurance			
Maintenance			
Taxes			

AUTO/TRAVEL EXPENSES	EXPECTED AMOUNT	ACTUAL AMOUNT	DIFFERENCE
Car Payment(s)			
Insurance			
Maintenance			
Fuel			
Mass Transit Passes			
Toll Expenses			

HOUSEHOLD EXPENSES	EXPECTED AMOUNT	ACTUAL AMOUNT	DIFFERENCE
Electricity			
Gas			
Water			
Trash/Recycling			
Cable/Internet Services			
Phone Services			
Credit Cards/Debt			
Loans			
Childcare			
Groceries			
Eating Out			
Entertainment			
Clothing			
Giving			

UPCOMING EXPENSES

month by month

JANUARY	FEBRUARY	MARCH

APRIL	MAY	JUNE

JULY	AUGUST	SEPTEMBER

OCTOBER	NOVEMBER	DECEMBER

monthly ← FINANCIAL GOALS

- ○ _____
- ○ _____
- ○ _____
- ○ _____
- ○ _____
- ○ _____
- ○ _____
- ○ _____
- ○ _____
- ○ _____
- ○ _____
- ○ _____
- ○ _____

yearly FINANCIAL GOALS

- ○
- ○
- ○
- ○
- ○
- ○
- ○
- ○
- ○
- ○
- ○
- ○
- ○

BILL PAYMENT *tracker*

ACCOUNT/BILL	DUE DATE	AMOUNT PAID	BALANCE	PAID

BANK ACCOUNT *information*

ACCOUNT #1

Financial Institution:_____ Account Type: _____

Account Number:_____ Routing Number:_____

User ID: _____ Password: _____

Card Number: _____ Pin: _____

Name(s) on Account:_____

Notes:_____

ACCOUNT #2

Financial Institution:_____ Account Type: _____

Account Number:_____ Routing Number:_____

User ID: _____ Password: _____

Card Number: _____ Pin: _____

Name(s) on Account:_____

Notes:_____

ACCOUNT #3

Financial Institution:_____ Account Type: _____

Account Number:_____ Routing Number:_____

User ID: _____ Password: _____

Card Number: _____ Pin: _____

Name(s) on Account:_____

Notes:_____

ACCOUNT #4

Financial Institution:_____ Account Type: _____

Account Number:_____ Routing Number:_____

User ID: _____ Password: _____

Card Number: _____ Pin: _____

Name(s) on Account:_____

Notes:_____

DEBT TRACKER
paydown worksheet

Account Name: _____   Account Number: _____

DATE	BEGINNING BALANCE	MIN. PAYMENT REQ.	AMOUNT PAID	REMAINING BALANCE

HOLIDAY BUDGET *planner*

GIFTS	ESTIMATED AMOUNT	ACTUAL AMOUNT	DIFFERENCE
Significant Other			
Kids			
Other Family Members			
Friends			
Coworkers			
Teachers			
Neighbors			
Hostess Gifts			

FOOD	ESTIMATED AMOUNT	ACTUAL AMOUNT	DIFFERENCE
Baking			
Holiday Meals			
Eating Out			
Entertaining			

DECOR	ESTIMATED AMOUNT	ACTUAL AMOUNT	DIFFERENCE
Indoor Decor			
Outdoor Decor			

TRAVEL	ESTIMATED AMOUNT	ACTUAL AMOUNT	DIFFERENCE
Lodging			
Transportation			
Meals			

CORRESPONDENCE	ESTIMATED AMOUNT	ACTUAL AMOUNT	DIFFERENCE
Cards			
Thank-You Notes			
Postage			

MISCELLANEOUS	ESTIMATED AMOUNT	ACTUAL AMOUNT	DIFFERENCE

STRAIGHTENING UP YOUR CLEANING

Does the phrase "organizing your cleaning" seem a bit redundant? It does to me, too. But, when your cleaning schedule is mapped out and your products are well-organized, this chore doesn't have to be such a dreaded one. This chapter is full of good, clean fun. It includes daily, weekly, monthly and deep-cleaning schedules and checklists, along with task lists for each cleaning zone in your home. I also tucked in a couple of chore charts to get all of your people motivated. And lots of labels, because labeling is half the fun (or battle, however you choose to look at it).

(continued)

four

STRAIGHTENING UP
YOUR CLEANING (CONT.)

DAILY CLEANING → *schedule*

THE KITCHEN	NOTES	COMPLETED	NOT DONE
wash dishes			
clean sink			
take out the trash			
wipe down countertops			
wipe down cooking surfaces			
wipe down table/bar			
sweep floors			

THE BATHROOM(S)	NOTES	COMPLETED	NOT DONE
wipe countertops			
wipe sink/fixtures			
wipe toilet seat			
spray shower with daily cleaner or vinegar			

THE BEDROOM(S)	NOTES	COMPLETED	NOT DONE
make beds			
straighten surfaces			
put away clothing			

LIVING AREA	NOTES	COMPLETED	NOT DONE
remove clutter			
fold throw blankets			
straighten throw pillows			
vacuum or sweep as needed			

UTILITY ROOM/MISCELLANEOUS	NOTES	COMPLETED	NOT DONE
straighten and deal with mail/papers			
do the laundry			
sweep porch			

WEEKLY CLEANING schedule

THE KITCHEN	NOTES	DAY COMPLETED	NOT DONE
wipe inside and outside of refrigerator			
dispose of old food (or compost)			
wipe down all appliances			
disinfect surfaces			
sweep and mop			
wipe baseboards			
dust blinds			
run cleaning cycle on coffee pot			

THE BATHROOM(S)	NOTES	DAY COMPLETED	NOT DONE
wipe and disinfect countertops and sink(s)			
clean and disinfect toilet, shower and tub			
sweep and mop			
wash rugs and linens			
empty trash			

THE BEDROOM(S)	NOTES	DAY COMPLETED	NOT DONE
wash and change sheets			
dust all surfaces and blinds			
vacuum, wipe baseboards			

LIVING AREA	NOTES	DAY COMPLETED	NOT DONE
vacuum furniture/window treatments			
fold blankets and straighten throw pillows			
dust all surfaces			
vacuum, sweep, mop, wipe baseboards			

UTILITY ROOM/MISCELLANEOUS	NOTES	DAY COMPLETED	NOT DONE
wipe washer/dryer			
sweep porch			
wash rugs, sweep, mop, wipe baseboards			

MONTHLY CLEANING
schedule

THE KITCHEN	NOTES	COMPLETED	NOT DONE
wipe blinds with cleaner			
wash windows			
wipe down cabinetry			
clean coils on refrigerator			
clean oven			
clean vent/hood			
wash and disinfect trash can			
wipe down pantry shelves			

THE BATHROOM(S)	NOTES	COMPLETED	NOT DONE
remove and clean showerhead			
wash windows			
wash and disinfect trash can			
dust light fixture			
wipe down cabinetry			

THE BEDROOM(S)	NOTES	COMPLETED	NOT DONE
clean out drawers and shoes			
wash windows			
wipe blinds with cleaner			

LIVING AREA	NOTES	COMPLETED	NOT DONE
clean electronics			
clean fan(s)			
wash throw blankets/pillows			
steam clean carpets/rugs			

UTILITY ROOM/MISCELLANEOUS	NOTES	COMPLETED	NOT DONE
clean insides of washer/dryer			
wash windows			
power spray outdoor surfaces			

_____'s
CHORE CHART

task/chore	s	m	t	w	t	f	s

_____'s

CHORE CHART

task/chore	s	m	t	w	t	f	s

KEEP

DONATE

MOVE TO ANOTHER SPACE

TRASH

Clutter Sorting Labels

five

WHIPPING YOUR KITCHEN INTO SHAPE

The heart of the home or the heart of the mess? My best bet to keeping things running smoothly in my kitchen is to keep it as organized as I can, which helps the daily kitchen clean up go easily, too. This chapter is well-stocked with fill-in menu planners, grocery lists and more.

KITCHEN CONVERSIONS 87

Place this handy chart on the inside of a cabinet door or frame it for a countertop. It's perfect for easy reference when you're working on a recipe. Whether doubling, tripling or creating your own recipes, this is an invaluable tool for any home cook.

METRIC KITCHEN CONVERSIONS 88

Nowadays, we use more than just a traditional recipe book for a meal. The Internet makes it easy to prepare a recipe from the other side of the world. Keep this handy chart nearby to make conversions easy.

MONTHLY MEAL PLANNING 89

Planning meals a month in advance makes life a little easier in the dinner department. Using this planner to keep track of your leftovers and meals in the freezer you plan to use is super helpful, too.

ON THE MENU (WITHOUT GROCERY LIST) 91

On my blog, my menu designs are my most downloaded resource. Use this chart to know what you'll be eating for the next week ahead—and it's great for the kids to refer to as well. Be sure to plan those nights out, too!

ON THE MENU (WITH GROCERY LIST) 93

While super similar to the regular menu print, this one has space to jot down groceries that may be needed for a specific recipe. You can even bring it to the store with you!

GROCERY LIST-DON'T FORGET A THING 95

Organizing your grocery list by department makes shopping a breeze! It's also helpful to keep this print near the pantry for staple shortages. This is another good one to laminate and use with a fine tip dry-erase marker.

(continued)

five

WHIPPING YOUR KITCHEN INTO SHAPE (CONT.)

Kitchen Conversions

DRY MEASUREMENTS

1 cup	= 16 tbsp	= 48 tsp	= 250 ml
3/4 cup	= 12 tbsp	= 36 tsp	= 175 ml
2/3 cup	= 10+2/3 tbsp	= 32 tsp	= 150 ml
1/2 cup	= 8 tbsp	= 24 tsp	= 125 ml
1/3 cup	= 5+1/3 tbsp	= 16 tsp	= 75 ml
1/4 cup	= 4 tbsp	= 12 tsp	= 50 ml
1/8 cup	= 2 tbsp	= 6 tsp	= 30 ml
1/16 cup	= 1 tbsp	= 3 tsp	= 15 ml

LIQUID MEASUREMENTS

1 gallon	= 4 quarts	= 8 pints	= 16 cups	= 128 ounces
1/2 gallon	= 2 quarts	= 4 pints	= 8 cups	= 64 ounces
1/4 gallon	= 1 quart	= 2 pints	= 4 cups	= 32 ounces
1/8 gallon	= 1/2 quart	= 1 pint	= 2 cups	= 16 ounces
1/16 gallon	= 1/4 quart	= 1/2 pint	= 1 cup	= 8 ounces

Metric Kitchen Conversions

LIQUID MEASUREMENTS

PINTS	METRIC	CUPS	FL. OZ.
n/a	100 ml	n/a	3 1/2
n/a	125 ml	1/2	4 1/2
1/4	. 150 ml	n/a	5
n/a	200 ml	n/a	7
n/a	250 ml	1	9
1/2	275 ml	n/a	10
n/a	300 ml	n/a	11
n/a	400 ml	n/a	14
n/a	500 ml	2	18
1	570 ml	n/a	20
n/a	750 ml	3	26
1 3/4	1.0 L	4	35
n/a	1.3 L	5	46
n/a	2.0 L	8	70

SPOON MEASUREMENTS

1 teaspoon= 5 ml

1 tablespoon= 15 ml

3 teaspoons= 1 tablespoon

WEIGHTS

IMPERIAL	METRIC	IMPERIAL	METRIC
1/2 oz	15 g	10 oz	285 g
3/4 oz	20 g	11 oz	310 g
1 oz	30 g	12 oz	340 g
2 oz	60 g	13 oz	370 g
3 oz	85 g	14 oz	400 g
4 oz	115 g	15 oz	425 g
5 oz	140 g	16 oz	450 g
6 oz	170 g	24 oz	680 g
7 oz	200 g	32 oz	0.9 kg
8 oz	230 g	48 oz	1.4 kg
9 oz	255 g	64 oz	1.8 kg

OVEN TEMPS

F	C
250	120
275	140
300	150
325	170
350	180
375	190
400	200
425	220
450	230

Monthly Meal Planning

ON THE MENU

Sunday
_____

Monday
_____

Tuesday
_____

Wednesday
_____

Thursday
_____

Friday
_____

Saturday
_____

ON THE MENU

Grocery List

Sunday

Monday

Tuesday

Wednesday

Thursday

Friday

Saturday

GROCERY LIST

don't forget a thing

FRUITS & VEGETABLES

BAKERY

DELI

DAIRY

MEAT MARKET

FROZEN

DRY GOODS

CANNED GOODS

SPICES & BAKING

SAUCES & CONDIMENTS

BEVERAGES

MISCELLANEOUS

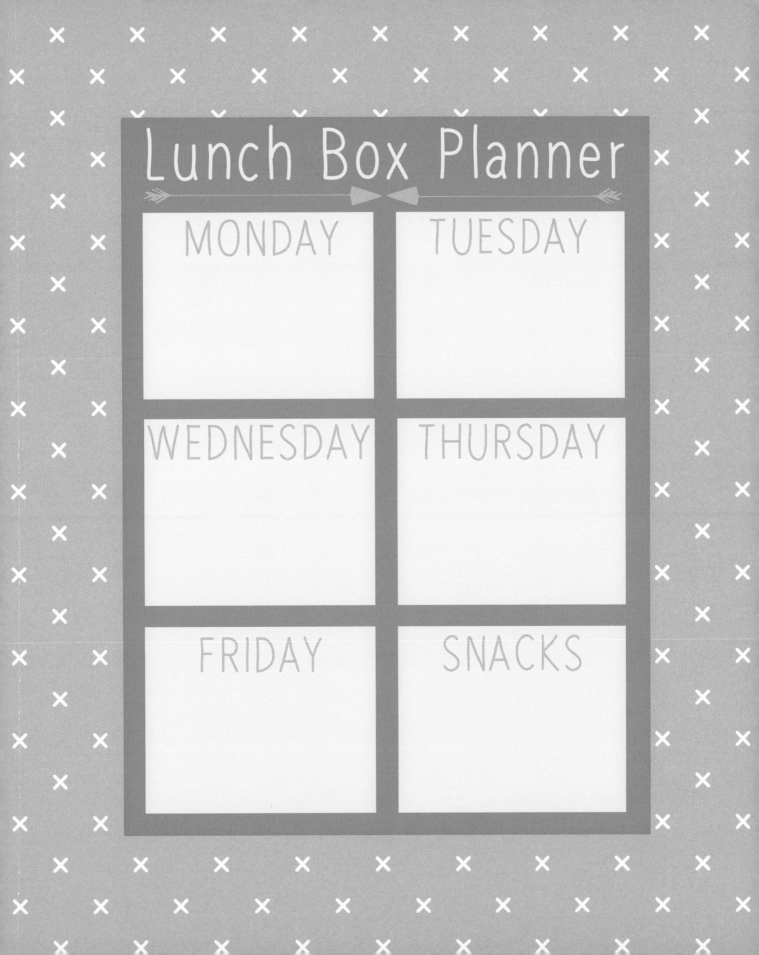

Lunch Box Planner

MONDAY

TUESDAY

WEDNESDAY

THURSDAY

FRIDAY

SNACKS

FREEZER INVENTORY

item	#	item	#

FRIDGE INVENTORY

item	#	item	#

PANTRY INVENTORY

item	#	item	#

white sugar

brown sugar

flour

wheat flour

cake flour

powdered sugar

nuts

dried fruit

baking chips

oats

dry cereal	hot cereal
oatmeal	granola
trail mix	coffee
tea	sweetener
hot cocoa	marshmallows

Pantry Labels

white rice	brown rice
pasta	quinoa
couscous	chips
pretzels	salty snacks
sweet snacks	cookies

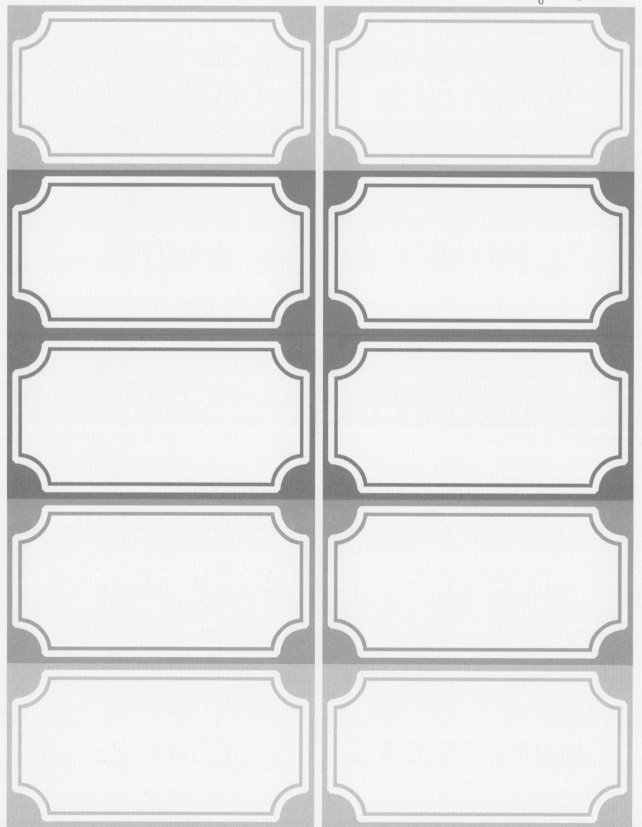

allspice	anise	bay leaves
cayenne pepper	celery seed	chili powder
cinnamon	cloves	coriander
cream of tartar	cumin	curry powder
dill weed	fennel seed	five spice powder
garlic powder	ground ginger	ground mustard
herbes de provence	nutmeg	seafood seasoning
onion powder	oregano	paprika
pepper, black	pepper, white	peppercorns
red pepper flakes	saffron	salt, kosher
salt, sea	seasoned salt	sesame seeds
tarragon	thyme	turmeric

Recipe Cards

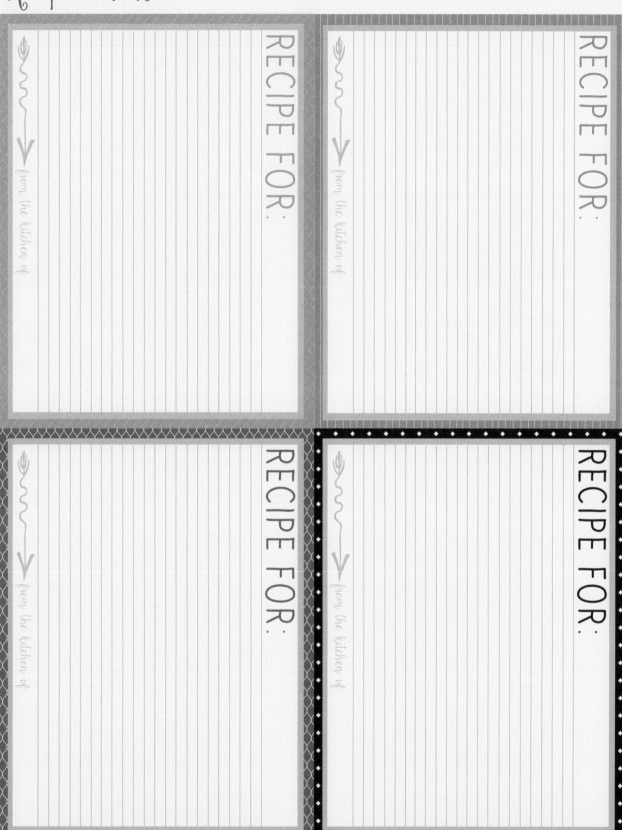

RECIPE FOR:

from the kitchen of

RECIPE FOR:

from the kitchen of

RECIPE FOR:

from the kitchen of

RECIPE FOR:

from the kitchen of

PLASTIC

PAPER

METAL

GLASS

six

HARMONIZING YOUR BATHROOM

Bathrooms are another area of the home that can become disorganized fairly quickly, especially with shared bathrooms. From medicine cabinet checklists to labels, this chapter will help those icky-prone bathrooms have a lot less ick in them. Be sure to check out the bathroom cleaning sections on the Daily, Weekly and Monthly Cleaning Schedules (page 75, 77 and 79).

MEDICINE CABINET INVENTORY

item	expires on	item	expires on
ACETAMINOPHEN			
ALLERGY MEDICINE			
ALOE VERA			
ANITIHISTAMINE MEDICATION			
ANITIHISTAMINE CREAM			
ANTACIDS			
ANTIBIOTIC OINTMENT			
ANTIDIARRHEAL			
ANTIFUNGAL MEDICINE			
ASPIRIN			
BANDAGES	-		
CALAMINE LOTION			
COLD AND FLU MEDICINE			
COUGH SUPPRESSANT			
DECONGESTANT			
EXPECTORANT			
EYE DROPS			
HEATING PAD	-		
HYDROCORTISONE CREAM			
IBUPROFEN			
LAXATIVES			
PETROLEUM JELLY			
SALINE SOLUTION			
THERMOMETER	-		
THROAT LOZENGES			
TWEEZERS	-		
YEAST INFECTION MEDICINE			

allergy

cold & flu

stomach

pain

vitamins & supplements

prescriptions

children's medicines

first aid

medicine cabinet labels

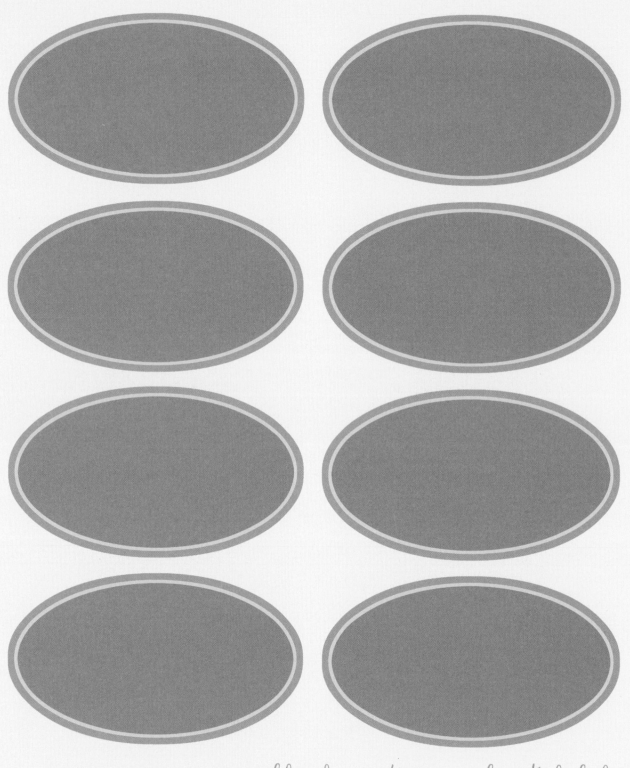

blank medicine cabinet labels

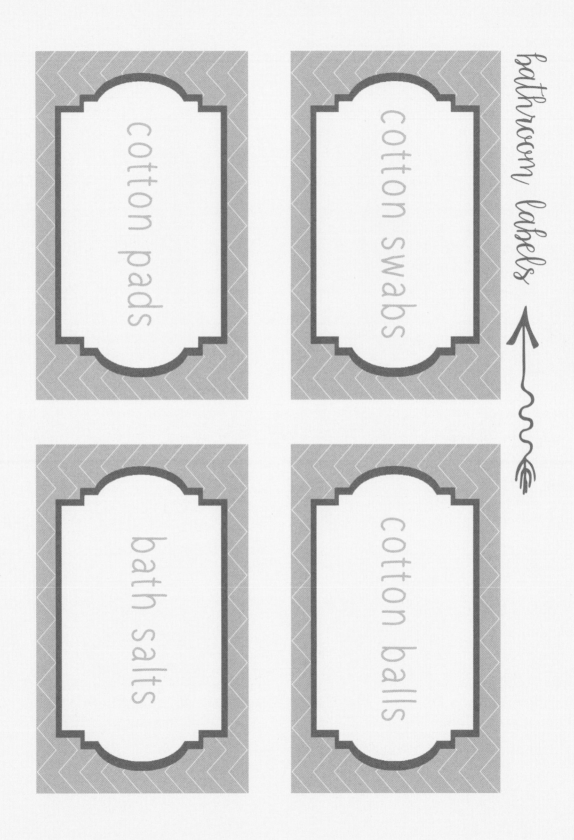

cotton pads

cotton swabs

bath salts

cotton balls

bathroom labels

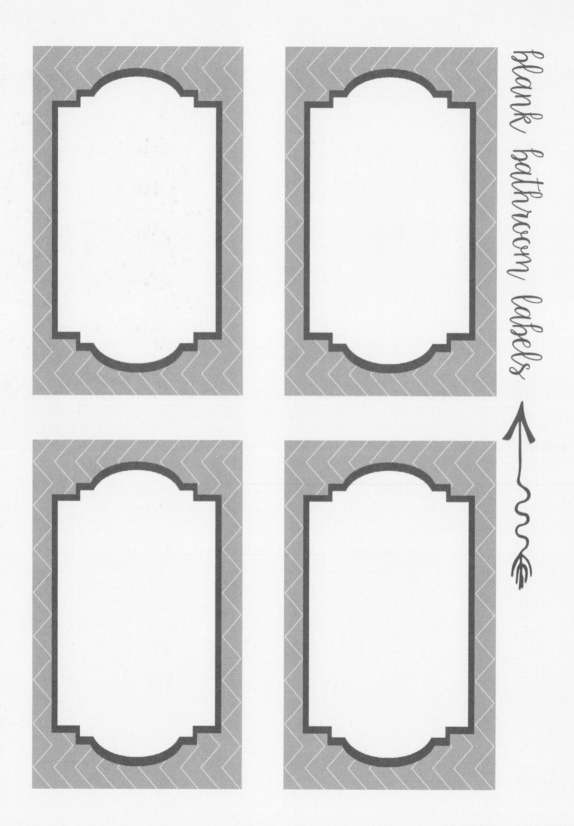

blank bathroom labels

TIDYING UP CHILDREN'S SPACES

Instilling a love (or even like) for organization in children can be a toughie. Simple steps and routines can help them to feel a part of the home-keeping process, whether it's in their own bedroom or a shared play space. This colorful chapter has lists, labels and other fun organizational prints geared to the little ones' spaces.

CHILDREN'S TOY LABELS

Once you have kiddos, their sheer magnitude of "stuff" can easily take over a room—or almost a home! One of the biggest storage needs in our home is always toys. Keeping toys under control and organized gives mom and dad their sanity back. These labels have visual art on them for kiddos who aren't at the reading age yet. There is also a blank set of labels for you to fill in as well. Cut out and use clear packing tape to seal these to toy boxes.

OUTDOOR TOY LABELS

I taught preschool for a year (it's not my gift, friends, but I did try!). One of the biggest things I learned that year was that children were more apt to enjoy toys that were organized. That extends to their outdoor gear, too. There's also a set of blank labels for your own needs. Copy, cut out and attach these to baskets or tubs with tape, twine or rope.

CHILDREN'S BOOKPLATES

Books were made for sharing, right? Swapping books with neighbors and friends is like your own little personal library. Be sure to label all of your kiddo's books so they always get back to you after your friends' children have enjoyed them. Make a copy of these to use them in all of your books—even grown-ups' books wouldn't mind a cute bookplate!

CHILDREN'S SCHEDULE CHART/PIECES

Make a copy of these and cut the pieces out. Laminate each piece and use magnets on the back. Write in your usual activities. These are perfect for kids to learn how their schedule works—they can move the pieces around as needed. This can also be left intact and framed for simplicity of use.

(continued)

seven

TIDYING UP
CHILDREN'S SPACES (CONT.)

PUZZLES

BLOCKS

CARS/TRUCKS

PLUSHIES

TRAINS

ELECTRONICS

DOLLS

ART SUPPLIES

GAMES

MUSICAL TOYS

BRICKS

PUPPETS

children's toy labels

blank children's toy labels

BALLS

SAND
TOYS

CHALK

WATER
TOYS

BUBBLES

CARS &
TRUCKS

→ *outdoor toy labels*

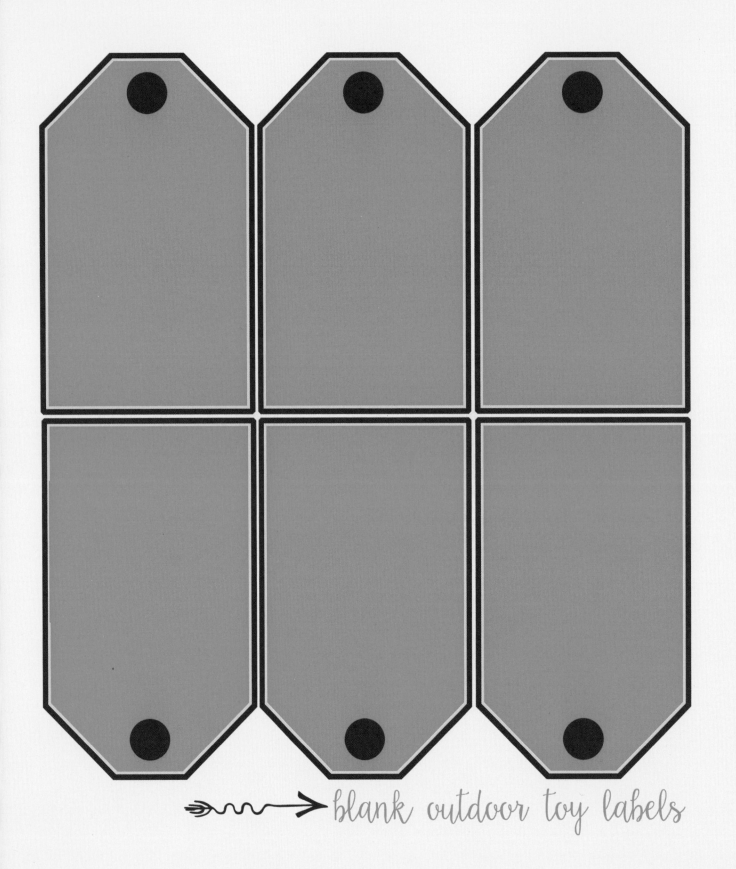

blank outdoor toy labels

Time	
7:00 AM	
8:00 AM	
9:00 AM	
10:00 AM	
11:00 AM	
12:00 PM	
1:00 PM	
2:00 PM	
3:00 PM	
4:00 PM	
5:00 PM	
6:00 PM	

children's schedule chart/pieces

comb your hair

get dressed

eat breakfast

brush your teeth

children's morning routine cards

take a bath

put on pajamas

brush your teeth

go to bed

children's evening routine cards

PRESCHOOL	PRESCHOOL
KINDERGARTEN	KINDERGARTEN
FIRST GRADE	FIRST GRADE
SECOND GRADE	SECOND GRADE
THIRD GRADE	THIRD GRADE
FOURTH GRADE	FOURTH GRADE
FIFTH GRADE	FIFTH GRADE
SIXTH GRADE	SIXTH GRADE
SEVENTH GRADE	SEVENTH GRADE
EIGHTH GRADE	EIGHTH GRADE
NINTH GRADE	NINTH GRADE
TENTH GRADE	TENTH GRADE
ELEVENTH GRADE	ELEVENTH GRADE
TWELFTH GRADE	TWELFTH GRADE
COLLEGE ADMISSIONS	COLLEGE ADMISSIONS
SCHOOL PICTURES	SCHOOL PICTURES
SPECIAL PROJECTS	SPECIAL PROJECTS
AWARDS & RECOGNITIONS	AWARDS & RECOGNITIONS
DIPLOMAS	DIPLOMAS

school papers file folder tabs

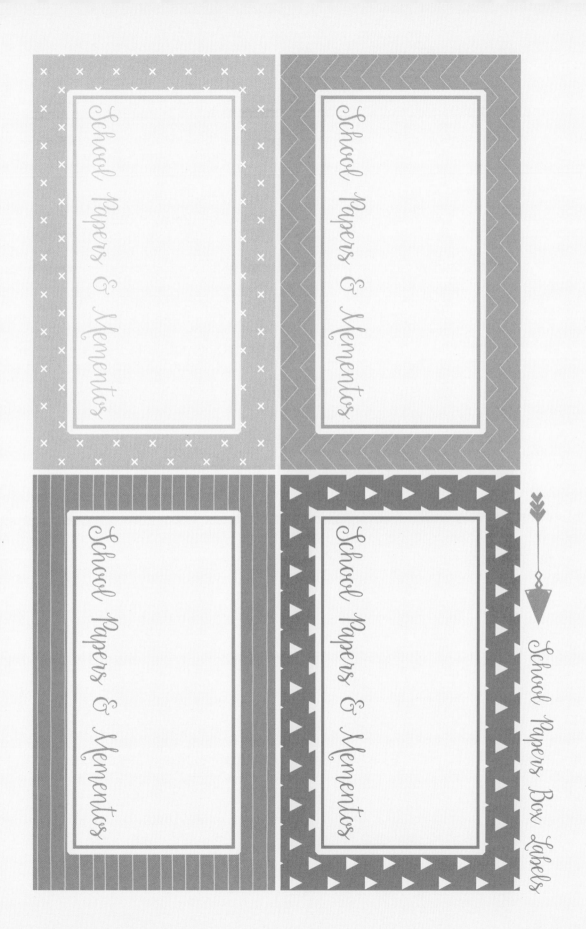

School Papers & Mementos

School Papers & Mementos

School Papers & Mementos

School Papers & Mementos

School Papers Box Labels

eight

TAILORING YOUR LAUNDRY ROOM

Oh laundry, the endless chore of—everyone. While you may or may not have an entire room dedicated to this chore, the prints in this chapter are designed to be used in any laundry space your lost socks (probably) call home. From helpful how-to lists for stains and basic laundry essentials, to colorful labels designed to make this task a little less monotonous—this is another squeaky-clean chapter.

LAUNDRY CARE
cheat sheet

WASHING

 machine wash

machine wash, *permanent press*

machine wash, *delicates*

 do not wash

 hand wash only

do not wring

 cool/cold

 warm

 hot

any bleach

non-chlorine bleach

do not bleach

DRYING

 any heat

 low heat

 medium heat

 high heat

 no heat

do not dry

 hang to dry

 dry flat

 drip dry

 dry in shade

 do not wring

IRONING

 low heat

 medium heat

 high heat

 do not iron

no steam

DRY CLEANING

 dry clean

 do not dry clean

quick guide to
STAIN REMOVAL AT A GLANCE

if you have this stain:	try this to remove it:
sauces	white vinegar
protein	baking soda
coffee stain	baking soda
red wine	white wine
cooking oil	dish soap
butter	cornstarch/dish soap
deodorant	denim
lipstick	baby wipes
perspiration	lemon juice
blood	hydrogen peroxide
ink	milk or hairspray
grass stain	white vinegar
crayon	olive oil

LAUNDRY
SOAP

DRYER
SHEETS

STAIN
TREATER

POCKET
FINDS

SAFETY
PINS

CLOTHES-
PINS

small laundry labels

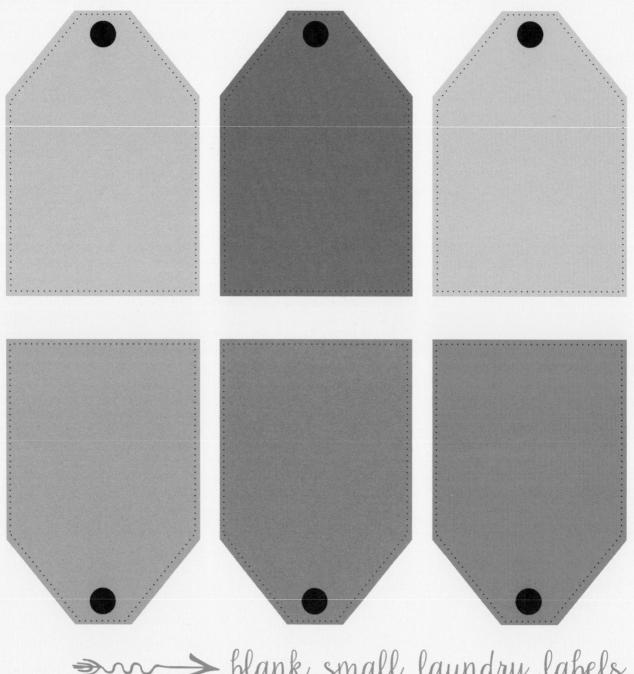

blank small laundry labels

nine

CATALOGING YOUR CLOSETS

Sometimes closets are the places where we stuff our stuff to allow the rest of the home to appear organized (been there, done that). But an organized closet makes getting ready for the day (or packing for a trip) a breeze—and pleasant! This chapter is filled with storage container labels, clothing dividers, closet inventory checklists and even linen closet storage prints.

BABY & TODDLER CLOSET DIVIDERS   151

Baby clothes sure aren't worn very long, are they? Between gifts and thinking ahead, new parents always seem to have clothing in a wide array of sizes for a newborn. These closet dividers make it simple to organize baby's closet by size. There's a blank set if you'd like to make some custom ones as well.

CHILDREN'S CLOSET DIVIDERS   153

One of the joys of parenting is when the kiddos start hanging up and putting away their own clothing. Having clothing dividers is super helpful in keeping them (and their closets) on track. These are a fabulous way to tackle a kids-clothing mess.

KIDS' DAILY CLOSET LABELS   157

On Sunday afternoon, as you stare at another week ahead, getting organized is one way to tackle it head on and win! Have kiddos pick out their clothing on Sunday for the entire week to avoid frustration and fuss on busy mornings. These dividers make it easy to keep clothes hanging up, while still "laid out" for the week. Just cut out and hang up. You can copy these onto cardstock for sturdier pieces.

CLOSET STORAGE LABELS   161

These labels will work with larger boxes in a closet for items like handbags and scarf collections. They coordinate with the shoe box labels to get a totally coordinated look in the closet.

(continued)

nine

CATALOGING
YOUR CLOSETS (CONT.)

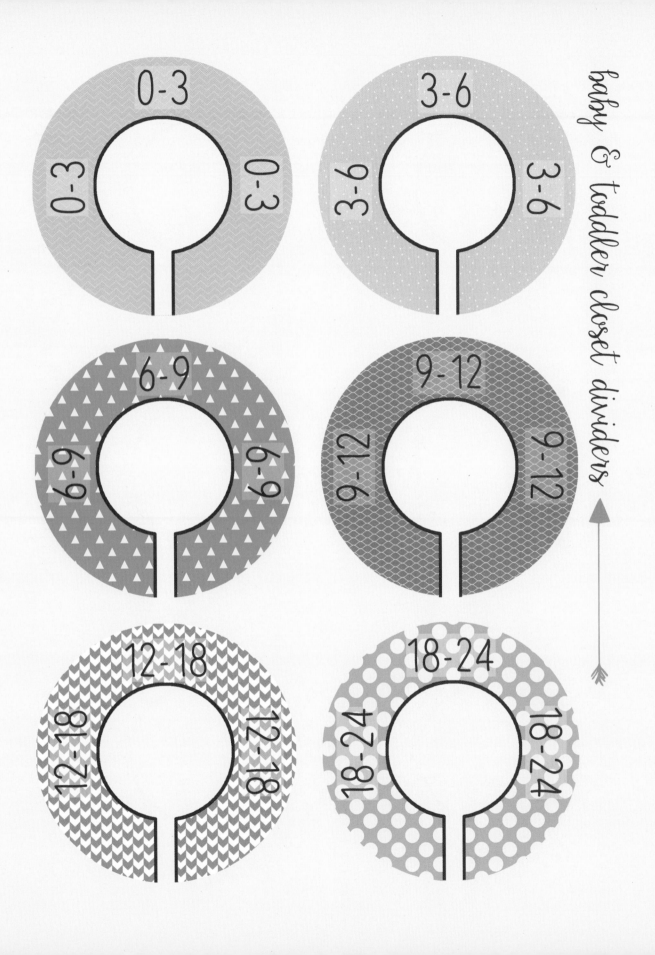

baby & toddler closet dividers

blank baby & toddler closet dividers

PANTS AND JEANS

SHORT-SLEEVE SHIRTS

LONG-SLEEVE SHIRTS

SWEATERS

SHORTS AND TRUNKS

SWEATSHIRTS AND HOODIES

children's closet dividers

PANTS AND LEGGINGS

SKIRTS AND SHORTS

DRESSES AND JUMPERS

SHIRTS AND TANKS

SWIMWEAR

CAPRIS AND JEANS

children's closet dividers

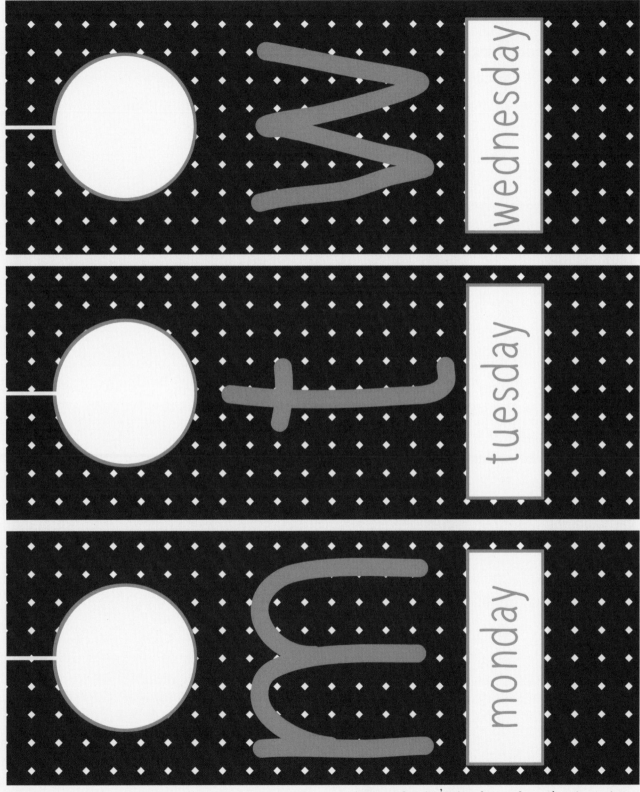

kids' daily closet dividers

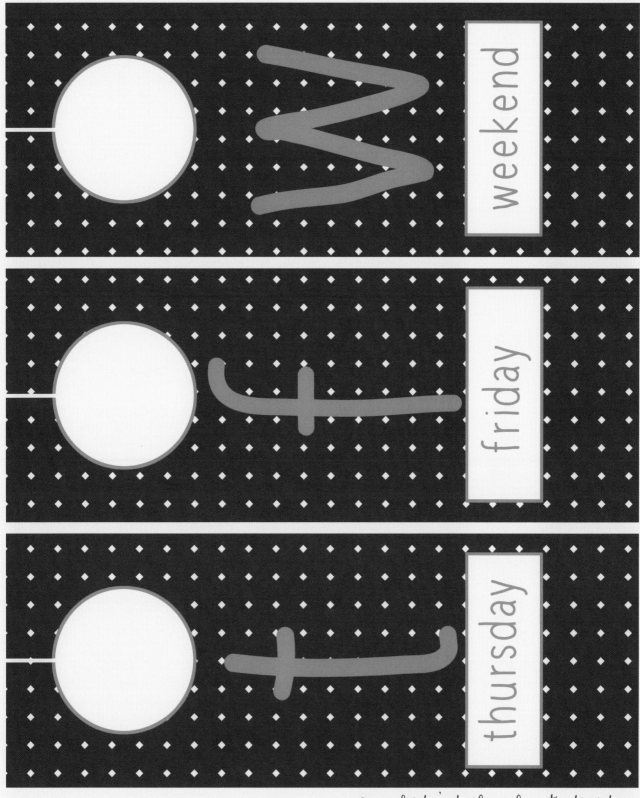

weekend

friday

thursday

kids' daily closet dividers

closet storage labels

shoe box labels

The clothing in this box belongs to:

size: | season:
○ ○ ○ ○
winter spring summer fall

The clothing in this box belongs to:

size: | season:
○ ○ ○ ○
winter spring summer fall

The clothing in this box belongs to:

size: | season:
○ ○ ○ ○
winter spring summer fall

The clothing in this box belongs to:

size: | season:
○ ○ ○ ○
winter spring summer fall

The clothing in this box belongs to:

size: | season:
○ ○ ○ ○
winter spring summer fall

The clothing in this box belongs to:

size: | season:
○ ○ ○ ○
winter spring summer fall

The clothing in this box belongs to:

size: | season:
○ ○ ○ ○
winter spring summer fall

The clothing in this box belongs to:

size: | season:
○ ○ ○ ○
winter spring summer fall

paints

brushes

glitter

stickers

stamps

glue

tape

decoupage

twine

ribbon

craft supply labels

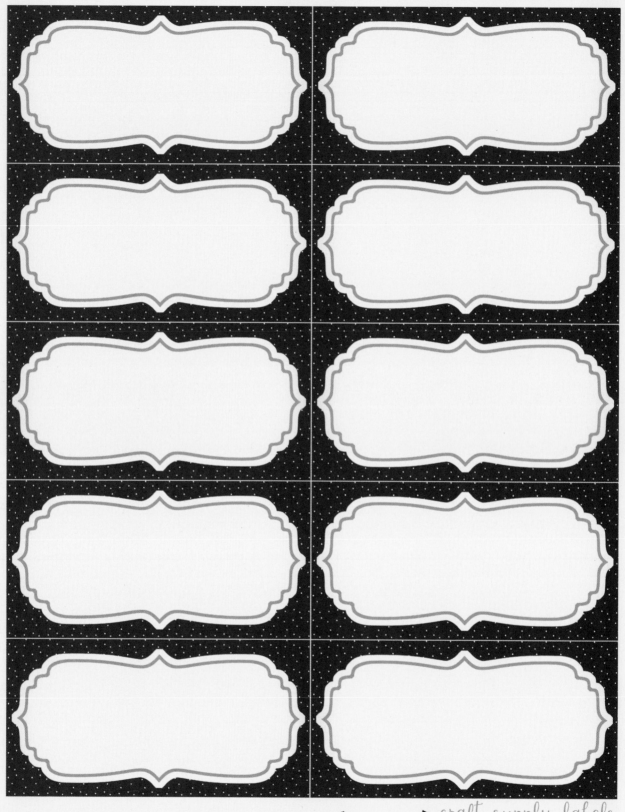

craft supply labels

WASHCLOTHS

HAND
TOWELS

BATH
TOWELS

BLANKETS

SHEETS

BEACH
TOWELS

linen closet labels

blank linen closet labels

ten

SHAPING UP YOUR GARAGE

It's tough being the neighbor with *that* garage (the one where the door never gets opened for the outside world to see in). But, with some simple cleanup and object organizing, parking a car in there can become a reality again. This chapter includes garage inventory checklists and loads of labels in a variety of sizes (for big and little toys and tools).

CONTENTS

CONTENTS

CONTENTS

CONTENTS

Small Storage Box Labels

CONTENTS

CONTENTS

CONTENTS

CONTENTS

CONTENTS

CONTENTS

CONTENTS

CONTENTS

CONTENTS

CONTENTS

paint can labels

paint
sample:

paint name:

finish: _____ year mixed: _____

where: _____

paint
sample:

paint name:

finish: _____ year mixed: _____

where: _____

paint
sample:

paint name:

finish: _____ year mixed: _____

where: _____

paint
sample:

paint name:

finish: _____ year mixed: _____

where: _____

HOLIDAY STORAGE

Holiday: _____
Contents: _____

_____
_____

HOLIDAY STORAGE

Holiday: _____
Contents: _____

_____
_____

HOLIDAY STORAGE

Holiday: _____
Contents: _____

_____
_____

holiday storage labels

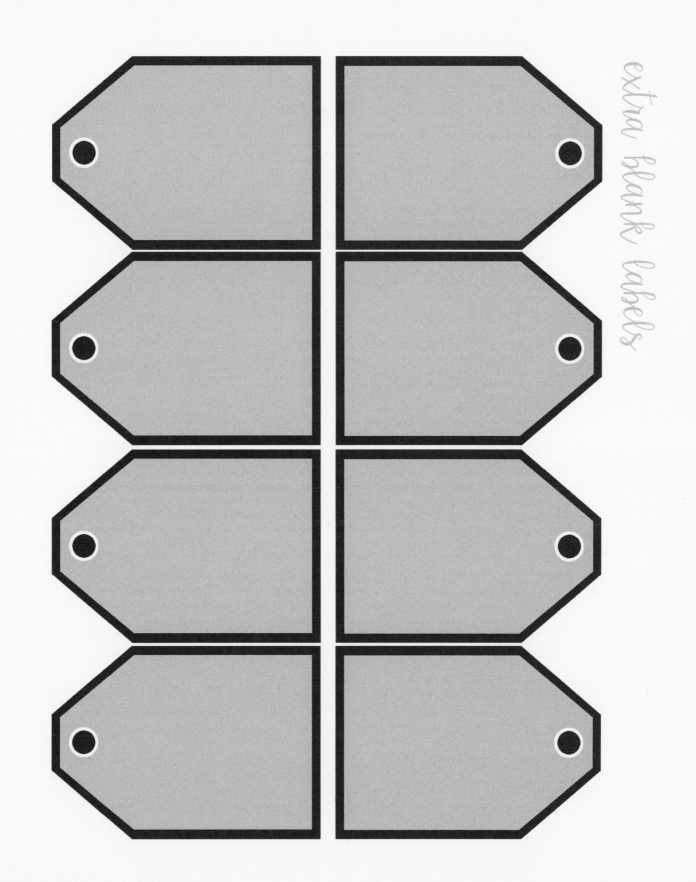

extra blank labels

extra blank labels

extra blank labels

ACKNOWLEDGMENTS

To David, for putting up with stressed-out days and design-block exhaustion. Thank you for being an encourager and spurring me on to accomplish dreams I never even knew I had.

To Benjamin, your neat-as-a-pin approach to life and all situations in an organized manner makes me smile...and wonder where on earth you got that from. Love ya.

To Jonathan, who told his entire class I was a book author before the ink on the contract was even dry: Your love of my work and bust-your-buttons proudness makes me tear up on a regular basis. You make me aspire to be as awesome as you truly think I am. xoxo.

To my parents who never put a cap on my dreams and always encouraged me to go further!

To my always remarkable friend and assistant, Gina: Thank you for your extra time in helping this book come together...working your fingers to the bone to make my dreams a reality. I'm truly grateful.

And to my blog readers and friends...thank you for being my favorite cheerleaders, ever.

ABOUT THE AUTHOR

Kristi Dominguez is the graphic designer, writer and mediocre perfectionist behind the blog I Should be Mopping the Floor. She has been a freelance graphic designer since 2003. Her love of design (both graphic and interior) morphed into a blogging career in 2011. A born-and-raised Texan, Dominguez is married to a high school principal and has two sons. Her relatable and down-to-earth designs have been featured in *Good Housekeeping, Country Living, Redbook* and the *Huffington Post*. Between chasing her boys and running a website, household organization became a necessity that she was able to achieve via her graphic design skills. She and her family currently reside in Harker Heights, Texas.

INDEX